EXTREME MACHINES

PLANES

DAVID JEFFERIS

W

FRANKLIN WATTS

LONDON • SYDNEY

First published in 2006 by
Franklin Watts
338 Euston Road
London NW1 3BH

Franklin Watts Australia
Hachette Children's Books
Level 17/207 Kent St,
Sydney, NSW 2000

EXTREME MACHINES: PLANES
Created for Franklin Watts by
Q2A Creative
Editor: Chester Fisher
Designers: Sudakshina Basu, Ashita Murgai
Picture Researcher: Jyoti Sethi

A CIP catalogue record for this book is
available from the British Library.

ISBN 0 7496 6320 0

Printed in China

Dewey number: 629.133'34

PICTURE CREDITS
Front cover: Stephen Fox, Back cover: Steve Flint
pp. 1 main (Riccardo Braccini-Aviopress), 4-5 bottom (Gabriele Macri), 5 top (Library of Congress,
LC-W861-35), 6–7 top (NASA), 6 middle (NASA), 7 bottom (NASA / Jim Ross),
8–9 top (Daniel Butcher), 9 bottom (Reuters), 10-11 bottom (Andreas Heilmann),
11 top (Bjorn van der Velpen), 12 top (Markus Herzig), 12 bottom (Riccardo Braccini-Aviopress),
13 middle (Yevgeny Pashnin), 14 right (NASA), 15 top (NASA), 15 middle (NASA),
16 bottom (U.S. Navy photo by Photographer's Mate 3rd Class Angel Roman-Otero),
16–17 top (Lockheed Martin Corporation), 18 middle (NASA/Nick Galante/PMRF),
19 right (Northrop Grumman), 20 top (NASA), 21 top (U.S. Air Force photo by Senior
Airman Stacey Durnen), 21 bottom (Chad Thomas), 22 bottom (Ben Wang), 23 top (Steve Flint),
24 top (Northrop Grumman), 24 bottom (Northrop Grumman), 25 bottom (NASA/Jim Ross),
26 top (Courtesy of Scaled Composites, LLC), 26 bottom (Courtesy of Scaled Composites, LLC),
27 top (Courtesy of Scaled Composites, LLC), 28 top left (Library of Congress, LC-W861-35),
28 middle right (NASA), 29 middle left (U.S. Navy photo by Photographer's
Mate 3rd Class Angel Roman-Otero), 29 top right (NASA).

CONTENTS

WEIRD WINGS

Mankind's experiments with powered flight began in the late 19th century, when many pioneers tried – and failed – to make a successful aircraft. Then, in 1903, the US Wright brothers, in their aircraft Flyer, made the first powered flight.

FLYING STEAMER

Before the Wright brothers flew into the history books, Frenchman Clement Ader had built a bat-winged plane called the Éole. It had a small steam engine and made a flight of just 50 metres (165 feet). However, the flight set no height records – most of it was just 20 centimetres (8 inches) above the ground! Even so, the 1890 flight was an important step in the history of flight.

THE WRIGHT FLYER

The Wright brothers became air enthusiasts after learning of other air pioneers. Their invention, Flyer, was the world's first true aircraft – power came from a small home-built petrol engine and the plane was steered successfully throughout its many flights. To steer, the pilot pulled cables that actually bent the wings up or down. Today, separate controls, called ailerons, do this.

Pilot sat in small cabin

Éole

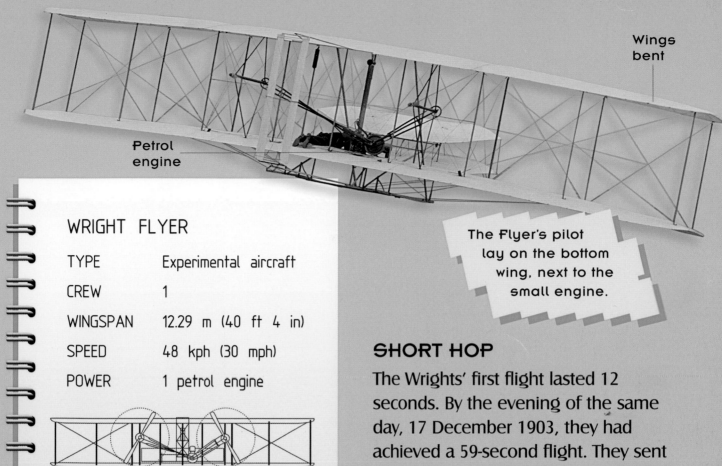

Wings
bent

Petrol
engine

The Flyer's pilot
lay on the bottom
wing, next to the
small engine.

WRIGHT FLYER

TYPE	Experimental aircraft
CREW	1
WINGSPAN	12.29 m (40 ft 4 in)
SPEED	48 kph (30 mph)
POWER	1 petrol engine

SHORT HOP

The Wrights' first flight lasted 12 seconds. By the evening of the same day, 17 December 1903, they had achieved a 59-second flight. They sent messages to confirm their success, but many newspaper editors did not believe the news at first! Even so, the brothers had done it and the air age had begun.

Éole did leave the
ground, but had no
proper steering controls.

Wood ribs
kept canvas
wings
stretched

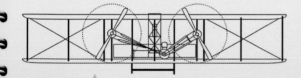

ADER ÉOLE

TYPE	Experimental aircraft
CREW	1
WINGSPAN	14 m (45 ft 11 in)
SPEED	24 kph (15 mph)
POWER	1 steam engine

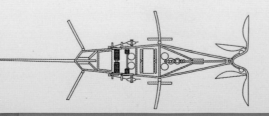

web

FINDER

http://www.flyingmachines.org/ ader.html
There is little detailed knowledge about Ader's experiments. This link is a good start.
http://www.first-to-fly.com/
Try this link for lots of information on the Wright brothers.

SPEED!

NASA

The X-43 looks like a paper dart! Its 3.65 m (12 ft) long fuselage (body) is covered with special materials to keep the insides cool during high-speed flight.

Since the dawn of powered flight in the early 20th century, many aircraft have been designed to reach top speeds. The first planes staggered through the air at only about 50 kph (31 mph) – today the record stands nearly 150 times faster!

Rocket motor in rear fuselage

The Bell X-1 was shaped like a bullet.

Single-seat cabin

6063

FASTER THAN SOUND

In 1947, the Bell X-1 was the first plane to fly faster than the speed of sound, Mach 1 or 1,062 kilometres/hour (660 miles/hour). This was a dangerous flight for Charles Yeager, the US pilot, as most planes at that time flew at little more than half this speed.

BELL X-1

TYPE	Rocket-powered research plane
CREW	1
WINGSPAN	8.53 m (28 ft)
SPEED	1,079 kph (670 mph); later versions flew faster
POWER	1 Reaction Motors rocket engine

Scramjet engine under fuselage

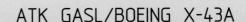

ATK GASL/BOEING X-43A

TYPE	Research vehicle
CREW	None
WINGSPAN	1.5 m (5 ft)
SPEED	11,270 kph (7,000 mph)
POWER	1 scramjet engine

A RECORD-BREAKING FLIGHT

In 2004, a US research plane called X-43 flew at 11,270 kilometres/hour (7,000 miles/hour). The X-43's experimental engine fired for just 10 seconds, but in that time the tiny craft hurtled more than 21 kilometres (13 miles) through the air! The record-breaking flight was made possible by a new type of engine called a 'scramjet'. This burns fuel in the airstream passing by, rather than inside the plane itself. Future scramjets promise even higher speeds.

A B-52 bomber carried the X-43 high into the air. Here it was dropped, then boosted to high speed by a Pegasus rocket.

FINDER

http://www.nasm.si.edu/research/aero/aircraft/bellx1.htm
Check out this site for more information on the Bell X-1.

JETLINERS

One jet engine under each swept wing

Two-crew flight deck

A Boeing 737 is made up of 367,000 parts.

BOEING 737

TYPE	Short/medium-range airliner
CREW	2, plus cabin crew
WINGSPAN	28.8 m (94 ft 9 in)
SPEED	908 kph (565 mph)
POWER	2 turbofan engines

Until the 1960s, most airliners were propeller-powered and flew quite slowly. Today all but the smallest passenger planes are powered by jet engines. Most are made by two companies, the US Boeing and the European Airbus.

A WORLD-BEATER

The Boeing 737 is far and away the most popular jetliner in the world. Since the plane's first commercial flight in 1968, more than 5,300 have been built. Over the years many versions have been made, all looking similar, but with different engines or seating more passengers – early 737s seated around 110, newer ones can fit 189!

AIRBUS A380

TYPE	Medium/long-range airliner
CREW	2, plus cabin crew
WINGSPAN	79.8 m (262 ft)
SPEED	903 kph (561 mph)
POWER	4 turbofan engines

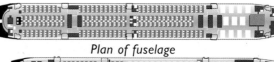

Plan of fuselage

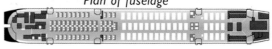

BIGGEST AIRLINER

The Airbus A380 is the largest jetliner ever built, seating about 555 passengers in a two-deck fuselage (three, if you count the cargo deck under the passengers). Fully-loaded with passengers, cargo and fuel, this air giant weighs up to 560 tonnes (1,234,589 lb) at take-off and can fly up to 12,880 kilometres (8,000 miles) without refuelling.

web

FINDER

http://www.boeing.com/commercial/737family/flash.html
This is Boeing's own site for its main breadwinner, the 737.
http://www.airbus.com/product/a380_backgrounder.asp
This is the Airbus site for the super-huge A380.

The Airbus A380 comes in airliner and freighter versions.

MEGALIFTERS

Most jetliners carry some cargo, usually stored under the passenger deck. Some planes, the megalifters, are built to carry outsize loads.

FLYING WHALE

The weird-looking Airbus A600ST Beluga was named after a kind of whale. It's well-named, for it looks very like the animal. The A600ST was designed as a flying truck, up to 41 tonnes (90,390 lb) of cargo being loaded through a lift-up door at the front, while the crew's flight deck slots in underneath. For all its awkward appearance, the A600ST is an amazingly agile flyer – at air shows, the plane regularly flies tight turns at angles that make your jaw drop!

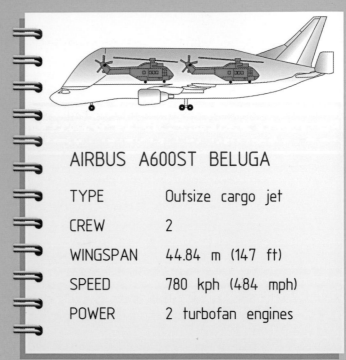

AIRBUS A600ST BELUGA

TYPE	Outsize cargo jet
CREW	2
WINGSPAN	44.84 m (147 ft)
SPEED	780 kph (484 mph)
POWER	2 turbofan engines

The A600ST's cargo door lifts up from the nose section.

Two jet engines

SIX-ENGINE ROCKET CARRIER

Russia's huge Antonov 225 was built in 1988, to carry the Buran, Russia's lookalike answer to the US space shuttle. Instead of being carried in a cargo hold, Buran was carried on the An-225's back!

Three engines under each wing

Loaded with cargo, people and fuel, the An-225 weighs up to 660 tonnes (1,455,051 lb).

Twin fins

UR-82060

BIGGEST CARGO JET

The An-225 was not a brand-new design. In fact, the plane was based on another cargo jet to which the designers added two more engines, a bigger wing and twin fins at the tail. Only one An-225 was built and it is still the biggest cargo jet ever flown.

Cargo door

Flight deck below nose

AN-225

TYPE	Super-heavy cargo jet
CREW	6, up to 70 passengers
WINGSPAN	88.4 m (290 ft)
SPEED	850 kph (528 mph)
POWER	6 turbofan engines

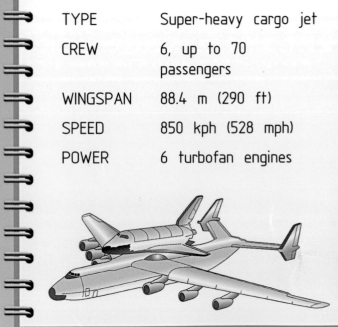

web

FINDER

http://flug-revue.rotor.com/FRTypen/FRBeluga.htm
Many Beluga details are shown at this German aviation site.
http://www.air-and-space.com/Antonov %20An-225%20Mriya.htm
Here you can see an enthusiast's pictures of the An-225.

WATER WINGS

A CL-415 drops a water load. This can be mixed with special foam, which helps to put out a fire quickly.

CANADAIR CL-415

TYPE	Amphibious water-bomber
CREW	2, plus seats for 9
WINGSPAN	28.6 m (93 ft 11 in)
SPEED	376 kph (234 mph)
POWER	2 turboprop engines

Some planes don't need to use a normal runway. They can also take off and land on water, because they have a waterproof boat-type hull as well as a normal undercarriage.

WATER BOMBER

The Canadair CL-415 is the world's only firefighting plane that is amphibious, meaning that it can operate from land or water. The CL-415 is built in Canada, a country that has vast forests where fires can rage in summer. The plane can carry 6,137 litres (1,352 gallons) at a time, and crews drop this load as a liquid 'bomb' that can stop a fire in its tracks. If there is a lake nearby, the CL-415 does not have to return to base. Instead, it skims along the surface, scooping up a full load of water in just 12 seconds.

WORLD'S FASTEST

The Beriev A-40 patrol plane comes from Russia and is still the fastest and largest amphibious plane, even though it first flew back in 1986. It has two jet engines, mounted high on the body to keep the air intakes well away from water spray. The A-40 was designed as a submarine-hunter. It can carry torpedoes and other weapons to drop on enemy subs.

The A-40 can also rescue people from crashed aircraft or sinking ships.

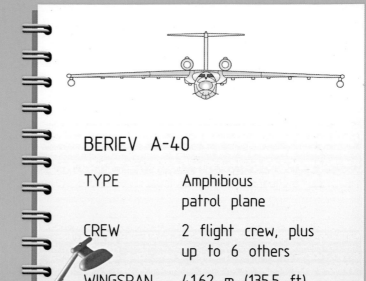

BERIEV A-40

TYPE	Amphibious patrol plane
CREW	2 flight crew, plus up to 6 others
WINGSPAN	41.62 m (135.5 ft)
SPEED	760 kph (472 mph)
POWER	2 turbofan engines

High-set 'T' tail

Two jet engines above the hull

Swept wing

The Beriev BE-12 Chaika [below], like the A-40, was designed as a submarine-hunter but has been adapted for firefighting.

FINDER

http://www.canadair.com/index.jsp
This is the home site of the company that makes the CL-415.
http://www.globalsecurity.org/military/world/russia/a-40.htm
Visit this site for some information on Russia's A-40.

X-PLANES

'X' stands for 'experimental', and over the years many weird-looking planes have been built to test the frontiers of flight.

BACK-TO-FRONT WINGS

The X-29 first flew in 1984 and at first glance looked much like a normal jet fighter. Once it was in the air, however, the wings showed it to be anything but normal. They were swept sharply forward, instead of pointing backwards. The X-29's designers thought the special wings would make it much more manoeuverable in flight. They were right, but the wings were too difficult to make in large numbers and so far the X-29 has stayed a one-off design.

Single-seat cockpit

Jet air intake

Wings made of super-stiff carbon-fibre material

GRUMMAN   X-29

TYPE   Forward-sweep X-plane

CREW   1

WINGSPAN   8.23 m (27 ft)

SPEED   1,931 kph (1,200 mph)

POWER   1 jet engine

Test pilot Chuck Sewell shows off the X-29's dramatic wing shape in flight.

The X-31 was flown for many years and some design features have been built into newer planes.

PADDLE POWER

The X-31 was another single-seater jet, this time with a triangular 'delta' wing shape and an air intake underneath the pilot's seat. Its unusual feature was tucked away at the tail, a trio of ultra-tough metal paddles that dipped in and out of the jet engine's powerful exhaust gases.

As the paddles angled, the jet thrust from side to side – so the X-31 twisted, turned and tumbled through the air. It flew at many air shows and thrilled the crowds with its dramatic flights, and was probably the most agile plane ever flown.

ROCKWELL/DEUTSCHE AEROSPACE X-31

TYPE	High-agility X-plane
CREW	1
WINGSPAN	7.21 m (23 ft 8 in)
SPEED	Mach 1.28+
POWER	1 turbofan engine

web

FINDER

*http://www.hq.nasa.gov/office/pao/
History/x1/programs.html*
This site gives an overview of early X-planes.
http://www.boeing.com/phantom/xplanesdt.html
Visit this site for info on latest X-planes.

JUMP JETS

The design of jump jets allows them to take off and land vertically, hover and speed through the air. This is achieved by changing the direction of the engine thrust.

WORLDWIDE FIGHTER

The most successful jump jet is the Harrier. The exhaust from its jet engine is directed by four nozzles, two on each side of the aircraft. When the pilot pulls a lever, the nozzles can swivel to point down for take off or landing, or be aimed backwards for speedy forward flight. The swivelling nozzles have made the Harrier an ultra-agile fighter that can beat much faster jets.

The Harrier has an unusual bicycle-style undercarriage. Most weapons are carried under the wings.

BAE SYSTEMS/
BOEING AV-8 HARRIER

TYPE	Jump-jet attack fighter
CREW	1 (plus 2-seat trainer version)
WINGSPAN	9.25 m (47 ft 1 in)
SPEED	1,065 kph (661 mph)
POWER	1 turbofan engine

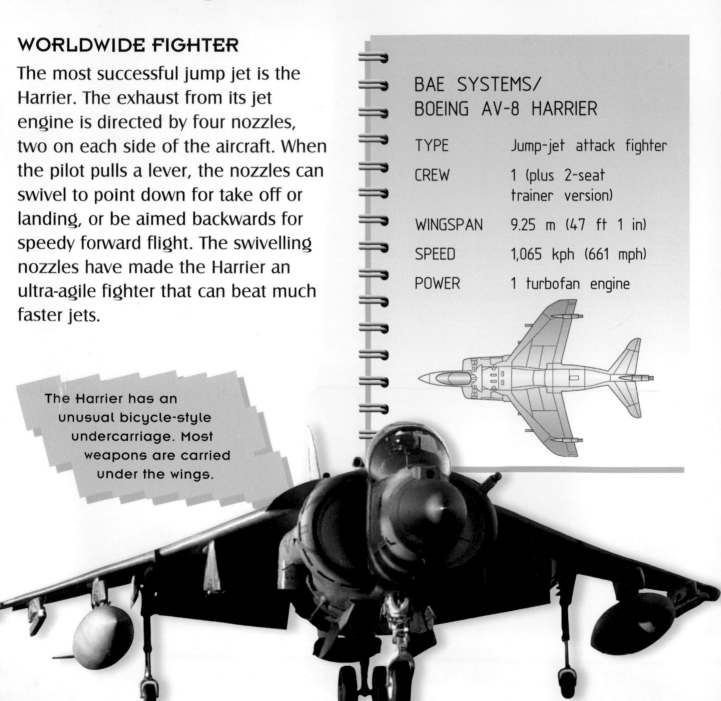

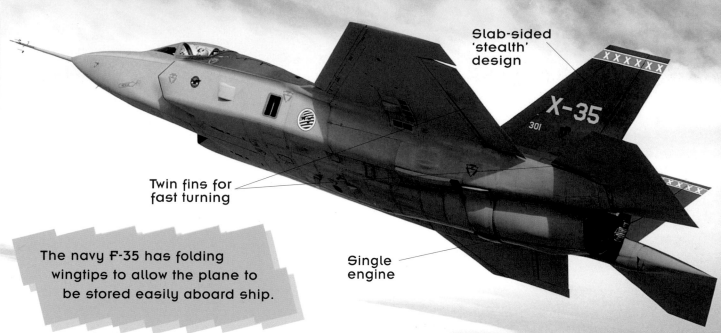

Slab-sided 'stealth' design

Twin fins for fast turning

Single engine

The navy F-35 has folding wingtips to allow the plane to be stored easily aboard ship.

AFTER THE HARRIER

The US F-35 was designed to replace the Harrier and is a huge worldwide aircraft project. Present plans call for nearly 5,000 F-35s to be built. The basic design comes in three kinds – an air-force fighter, a navy fighter and a special jump-jet version for the US Marines and the British Royal Navy.

FASTER AND FASTER

The F-35 will be bigger and faster than the Harrier – but it should be safer to fly as its stealth design will make it difficult for enemy radar to spot. It's an expensive project though, likely to cost more than $200 billion.

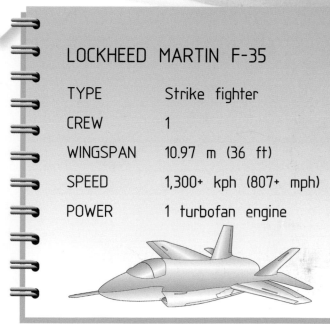

LOCKHEED MARTIN F-35

TYPE	Strike fighter
CREW	1
WINGSPAN	10.97 m (36 ft)
SPEED	1,300+ kph (807+ mph)
POWER	1 turbofan engine

web

FINDER

http://www.airforce-technology.com/projects/fa2/
This site gives details of the latest version of the Harrier.
http://www.lowobservable.com/F-35.htm
Visit this site for information on the F-35.

EXTREME MACHINES Planes

17

FLYING WINGS

In a normal plane, people and cargo are carried in the tube-shaped body, or fuselage. Flying wings have no fuselage, as everything is carried inside the wing itself.

ELECTRIC FLYER

The Helios flying wing was one of the most unusual aircraft built. Spanning an enormous 75.3 metres (247 feet), Helios was propelled by no less than 14 electric motors, powered by solar panels covering the top of the huge wing.

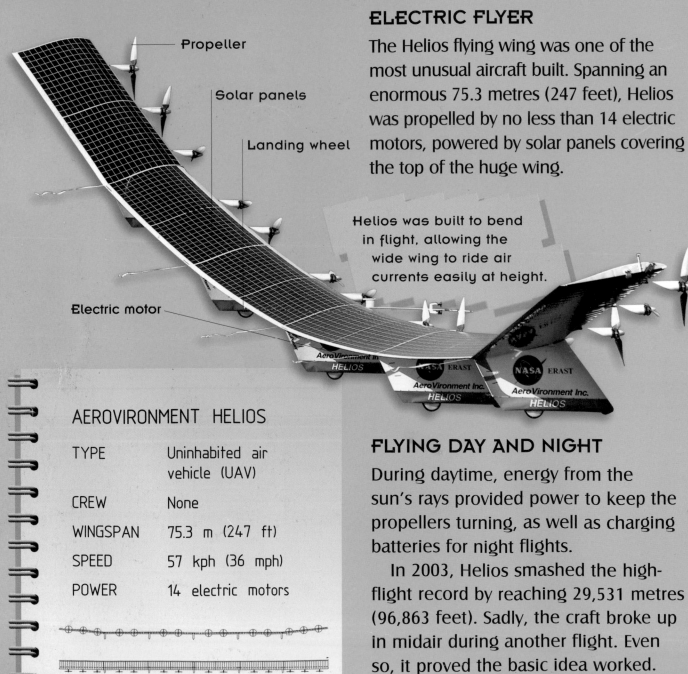

Propeller

Solar panels

Landing wheel

Electric motor

Helios was built to bend in flight, allowing the wide wing to ride air currents easily at height.

AEROVIRONMENT HELIOS

TYPE	Uninhabited air vehicle (UAV)
CREW	None
WINGSPAN	75.3 m (247 ft)
SPEED	57 kph (36 mph)
POWER	14 electric motors

FLYING DAY AND NIGHT

During daytime, energy from the sun's rays provided power to keep the propellers turning, as well as charging batteries for night flights.

In 2003, Helios smashed the high-flight record by reaching 29,531 metres (96,863 feet). Sadly, the craft broke up in midair during another flight. Even so, it proved the basic idea worked.

PRICEY PLANE

The US Air Force's B-2 bomber is the fastest and heaviest flying wing ever made. Fully loaded, it can weigh up to 170 tonnes (374,786 lb). It is also the most expensive bomber ever, at more than $2 billion (£1.1 billion) per aircraft.

Engines buried inside wing

Crew flight deck

NORTHROP-GRUMMAN B-2 SPIRIT

TYPE	Stealth bomber
CREW	2-3
WINGSPAN	52.43 m (172 ft)
SPEED	1,000 kph (600 mph+)
POWER	Four F118 turbofan engines

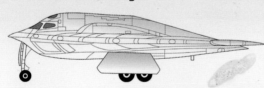

web

FINDER

http://www.is.northropgrumman.com/products/ usaf_products/b2/b2.html
B-2 maker's website
http://www.aerovironment.com/area-aircraft/ unmanned.html
Details of many UAVs

Northrop-Grumman B-2 Spirit's first flight was on July 17, 1989.

EXTREME MACHINES Planes

INVISIBLE PLANES

The SR-71 is still the jet speed record-holder, more than 40 years after its first flight.

Military pilots need to avoid being spotted by enemies, and flying high and fast is one way to avoid detection. Another way is to fly a 'stealth' plane, built of special materials to make it difficult to see on radar screens.

MIGHTY BLACKBIRD

The amazing SR-71 Blackbird was built to fly very high and very fast. It first flew in December 1964, yet still holds many height and speed records. In 1974 the plane flew across the Atlantic Ocean from New York to London – 5,585 kilometres (3,471 miles) – in less than two hours!

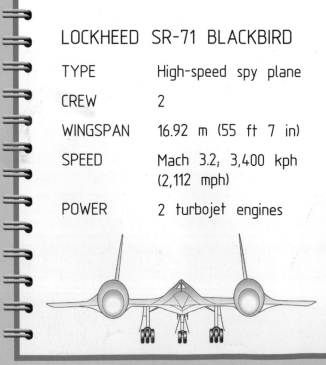

LOCKHEED SR-71 BLACKBIRD

TYPE   High-speed spy plane

CREW   2

WINGSPAN   16.92 m (55 ft 7 in)

SPEED   Mach 3.2; 3,400 kph
              (2,112 mph)

POWER   2 turbojet engines

STEALTHY SECRET

The weird-looking F-117 was the first combat plane to be designed from the outset as a 'stealth' jet. The strangely angled shape and special materials deflect and absorb enemy radar beams. Not surprisingly, the F-117 was kept secret for as long as possible – in fact, details were not revealed to the public until 1988, seven years after its first flight!

The F-117's pilot uses computer-controlled guidance systems to carry out an attack.

F-117 NIGHTHAWK

TYPE	Stealth ground-attack aircraft
CREW	1
WINGSPAN	13.2 m (43 ft 4 in.)
SPEED	1,040 kph (646 mph)
POWER	2 turbofan engines

FINDER

http://www.f22fighter.com
This site tells the history of the SR-71 and also features many pictures.
http://www.sr-71.org/aircraft/f-117.htm
Here you can check out the F-117 aircraft.

TOP GUNS

Top guns are the best pilots who fly the best fighter planes. The machines shown here are reckoned to be the deadliest aircraft in the sky.

SUPERCRUISER

The F-22 Raptor was designed with one aim in mind – to be the deadliest plane in the air. Its two engines give enough thrust (more than 35 tonnes!) to shoot the plane straight up after take-off, to more than 15,000 metres (50,000 feet) altitude. In level flight the F-22 can 'supercruise' – it can fly supersonic without any special engine boost, so it uses less fuel than other fighters.

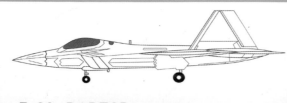

F-22 RAPTOR

TYPE	Stealth fighter
CREW	1
WINGSPAN	13.56 m (44 ft 6 in)
SPEED	1,483 kph (921 mph)
POWER	2 turbofan engines

The F-22 is the most expensive fighter today, at about $80 million US per plane.

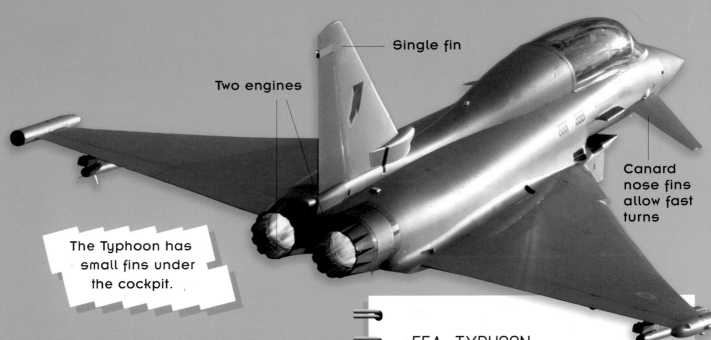

Single fin

Two engines

Canard nose fins allow fast turns

The Typhoon has small fins under the cockpit.

EUROPE'S TOP FIGHTER

The EFA Typhoon is Europe's most important combat jet, with four nations sharing the design and build – Britain, Germany, France and Spain. They claim the plane is the most advanced ever, though whether the F-22 or Typhoon would win in a midair battle is anyone's guess – they haven't tried yet, though friendly test-battles are likely in future!

VOICE CONTROL

Among the Typhoon's many features is its voice-control technology – the computers on-board can react to up to 200 commands spoken by the pilot, making the plane much easier to fly. Like the F-22, the Typhoon can also supercruise.

EFA TYPHOON

TYPE	Fighter and ground-attack
CREW	1 (2 for trainer version)
WINGSPAN	10.97 m (36 ft)
SPEED	Mach 2 at height
POWER	2 turbofan engines

web

FINDER

http://www.f22fighter.com
This site gives details of just about everything to do with the F-22.
http://www.eurofighter.com/Default.asp?Flash=True
This is the home site for the Typhoon.

ROBOT FLYERS

Satellite antenna under nose hump

V-shaped tail fins

U.S. AIR FORCE

Global Hawk has long, straight wings to help it cruise high above the Earth.

These planes are really 'extreme' – they don't even have a pilot aboard!

HUGE MACHINE

The giant Global Hawk is a spy-plane with a difference – it mostly flies itself, under the direction of on-board computers. The pilot-controller, back at base, changes height, direction or speed using a joystick similar to ones used in computer games.

SATELLITE SIGNALS

Information to and from the Global Hawk is sent via a satellite, orbiting in space far above. The plane can fly 20,000 metres (65,000 feet) above a

target for about 22 hours, recording events below in daytime, at night, or even through thick cloud. Global Hawk's cameras can spot objects as small as 30 centimetres (12 inches) across!

NORTHROP GRUMMAN
GLOBAL HAWK

TYPE	Uncrewed spy plane
CREW	None
WINGSPAN	35.4 m (116 ft 2 in)
SPEED	644 kph (400 mph)
POWER	1 turbofan engine

COMBAT ROBOT

The X-45 takes robotic flying another step forward – it is an experimental plane that can carry bombs or missiles to attack an enemy. Like the Global Hawk, on-board computers aboard the X-45 control its moment-to-moment flying, with changes in flight plan coming from pilot-controllers back at base.

PORTABLE PLANE

X-45 robo-bombers are quite small, have no tail-fin, and the wings can be taken off in a few minutes for storage. When the wings are off, an X-45 can be packed inside a container. In future, up to six robo-planes at a time could be taken by transport jet to a battle-zone airstrip.

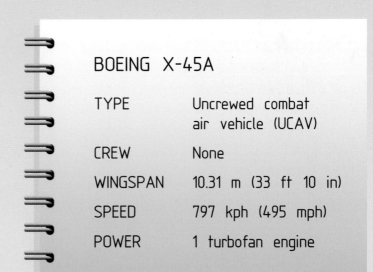

BOEING X-45A

TYPE	Uncrewed combat air vehicle (UCAV)
CREW	None
WINGSPAN	10.31 m (33 ft 10 in)
SPEED	797 kph (495 mph)
POWER	1 turbofan engine

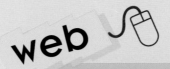

web

FINDER

http://www.boeing.com/defense-space/military/ x-45/x45media.html
This link takes you to an X-45 site with great pictures and videos.
http://www.is.northropgrumman.com/products/ usaf_products/global_hawk/global_hawk.html
Visit this site for information on Global Hawk.

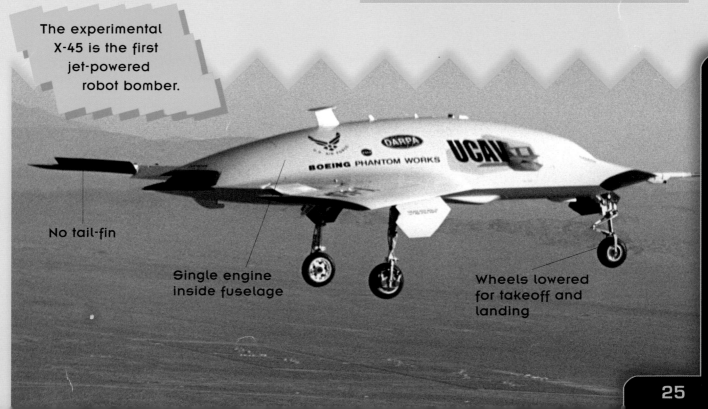

The experimental X-45 is the first jet-powered robot bomber.

No tail-fin

Single engine inside fuselage

Wheels lowered for takeoff and landing

THE EDGE OF SPACE

SpaceShipOne carried
underneath White Knight

White Knight's engines are
there for carrying power, not
speed – its maximum is less
than 300 kph (185 mph).

SCALED COMPOSITES
WHITE KNIGHT

TYPE	SpaceShipOne carrier plane
CREW	2
WINGSPAN	24.99 m (82 ft)
SPEED	298 kph (185 mph)
DROP SPEED	222 kph (138 mph)
POWER	2 jet engines

In 2004 a tiny rocket plane
became the first privately built
craft to reach the edge of space,
more than 100 kilometres
(62 miles) above the Earth.

BIG PRIZE

The Ansari X-Prize was an inspiration
for space enthusiasts – $10 million
to be won by the first private
team to fly a craft safely to the
edge of space, twice in two weeks.
Radical aircraft designer Burt Rutan
answered this challenge by creating
the tiny SpaceShipOne three-seater, to
be carried aloft by another Rutan design,
the jet-powered White Knight carrier plane.

WEIRD WINGS

SpaceShipOne looks simple enough, a bullet-shaped body with seats for three and a rocket motor at the back. Its unusual wings, invented by Rutan, made its amazing flight possible.

CARRIER PLANE

The white jet carrier plane was the twin to Rutan's X-Prize design. Looking like some prehistoric bird of prey, White Knight carried SpaceShipOne under its belly for take-off – climbing to a height of nearly 15,000 metres (50,000 feet).

SpaceShipOne hit a speed of 3,622 kph (2,250 mph) on its up-and-down flights high above the Earth.

RETURN TO BASE

Once at drop height, White Knight released SpaceShipOne, then returned to base in a flight totalling about 90 minutes. Meanwhile, SpaceShipOne's pilot fired up the rocket motor and flew straight up, in a soaring arc. At the top, he released some M&M sweets to float around the cockpit – after the rocket was turned off, everything in the craft became weightless for a few minutes!

SCALED COMPOSITES SPACESHIPONE

TYPE	Private rocket plane
CREW	1 (plus seats for 2 passengers)
WINGSPAN	4.98 m (16 ft 4 in)
SPEED	3,622 kph (2,250 mph)
POWER	1 rocket motor

web

FINDER

http://www.scaled.com/
This link takes you to SpaceShipOne's maker, Scaled Composites.
http://www.xprize.org/
Visit this site for information on the Ansari X-Prize.

TIMELINE

1903

First successful powered flight by the Wright brothers in their Flyer aircraft, on December 17. The first flight, with Orville Wright at the controls, lasted just 12 seconds. By sunset Orville and Wilbur had notched up three more flights, with a longest time of 59 seconds.

1914

First airline starts operations on New Year's Day, using a two-seat Benoist flying boat. The plane flew 35 km (22 miles), from St Petersburg to Tampa, in Florida. The ticket for the 23-minute journey was $5, with an extra charge if you weighed more than 91 kg (200 lb)! In all, 1,025 passengers used the airline, with only 22 cancelled flights – a good record because early engines were unreliable.

1927

First non-stop flight across the Atlantic Ocean, from New York to Paris. The pilot, Charles Lindbergh, flew alone on the 5,810-km (3,610-mile) trip. His plane was so extreme it didn't even include a windshield – the main fuel tank for the 33-hour flight was directly in front of the tiny cabin! To see out, Lindbergh used a mirror poking out of the side.

1935

First flight of the 28-seat Douglas DC-3, the most successful airliner ever. The twin-engine prop-plane was produced in dozens of different versions; some even had skis fitted! Military versions were also made during World War II – in all, more than 13,000 DC-3s were built and some still fly today.

1939

First flight of Germany's Heinkel He 178, the first jet plane, on August 27. The world's first combat jet was also German, the twin-jet Messerschmitt Me 262, which was more than 161 kph (100 mph) faster than anything else in the air.

1947

First supersonic flight by Bell X-1 rocket plane Glamorous Glennis, with pilot Charles Yeager at the controls. The X-1 was the first of many X-planes – the latest one is the X-45 UCAV and further designs are in the planning stages.

1949

First flight of the de Havilland Comet 1, the world's first jetliner. It entered passenger service with the airline BOAC four years later. Sadly, a number of crashes meant a big redesign and rival Boeing 707 became the big jetliner success of the 1950s and 1960s.

1960

First flight of the British P1127 jump jet, itself developed from the 'flying bedstead', a bizarre-looking machine used to test the engine. The P1127 became the Harrier combat jump jet, still flying today.

1969

First flight of the huge Boeing 747 jumbo jet, creating mass-market flying and the biggest jetliner made until the Airbus A380. A Boeing 747 had about 4.5 million separate parts, supplied by more than 1,500 companies around the world!

1991

First stealth aircraft flies. The F-117 Nighthawk resulted from research into the way radar works. It had special materials that soaked up some radar waves, and sharp angles to deflect others. Most new combat planes have stealth features.

1967

The X-15A-2 rocket plane flies at 7,274 kph (4,520 mph), still the record for a crewed rocket-plane flight. Like the X-1, the X-15 was flown to a great height by a carrier plane, then dropped in midair before firing its own rocket motor.

1986

First round-the-world flight without refuelling, by Jeana Yeager and Dick Rutan in the weird-looking Voyager, designed by Dick's brother Burt, who also designed SpaceShipOne. In storms, the plane's long wings flexed up and down, giving a sick-making ride – even so, the plane covered 40,252 km (25,012 miles) non-stop.

2004

First flight to the edge of space – 100 km (62 miles) – by the SpaceShipOne private rocket plane. Designer Rutan is working on a bigger version for regular passenger flights.

2005

First flight of the giant double-deck Airbus A380, the biggest jetliner in the world. Early A380s seat some 555 passengers, but bigger future versions may pack in 800 people or more.

GLOSSARY

AERODYNAMICS

The science or study of the forces acting on an aircraft in motion.

AFTERBURNER

A system that feeds raw fuel into a jet's hot exhaust, increasing thrust. It also increases fuel consumption.

AIRFRAME

Word for the structure of a plane, divided into various parts such as the fuselage (body), wings, tail unit and so on.

AMPHIBIOUS

A plane with wheels for runways and a sealed hull for use on water.

JUMP JET

A plane that can take off and land vertically. Jump jets such as the Harrier almost always use STOVL, which stands for Short Take Off, Vertical Land. The aircraft takes off over a short distance, but lands vertically.

LIFT

The force acting on an aircraft that keeps it in the air. Wings create lift.

MACH NUMBER

An aircraft's speed divided by the speed of sound.

PETROL ENGINE

An engine that uses the power of exploding petrol contained within cylinders to drive pistons and a crankshaft. This turns wheels or a propeller to power a vehicle forwards.

PROPELLER

In aircraft that are not jet-propelled, the assembly that spins around, creating thrust to drive the plane forwards.

RADAR

A type of sensor that sends out radio waves to detect objects. Radar beams bounce off the object and some of this is returned to the radar equipment, which shows this on a video screen.

ROBOTIC

Any machine that controls itself to a great degree. UAVs and UCAVs are robotic because they are mostly under the control of on-board computers, with human operators giving orders rather than actually doing the flying.

SATELLITE

A spacecraft that circles ('orbits') the Earth, sending out information. Satellites are often used for navigation, broadcasting or communications.

SCRAMJET

Experimental engine that burns fuel in the high-speed airflow, instead of inside the engine itself.

SENSOR

Any device that can sense objects around it, such as a microphone for sounds or a camera for vision.

SOLAR PANEL

Material that converts the energy in sunlight to electricity. Usually comes in very thin, flat panels.

STEALTH

Any plane designed from the outset to avoid detection by enemy radar. Stealth planes are built from materials that soak up radar energy. They are also shaped to deflect radar beams away.

STEAM ENGINE

An engine that uses steam created in a boiler to drive pistons to power a vehicle.

SUPERSONIC

Faster than the speed of sound, called Mach 1. At ground level, Mach 1 is about 1,226 kph (762 mph), High in the sky it is about 1,062 kph (660 mph). So, a high-flying plane travelling at Mach 1 is actually some 164 kph (102 mph) slower than a plane doing Mach 1 near the ground.

TORPEDO

Pencil-shaped underwater missile used to attack enemy ships or submarines. Torpedoes are sometimes dropped from aircraft.

TURBOFAN ENGINE

Type of jet engine with a big fan in front to suck in air. Uses much less fuel than the earlier and simpler engine, the turbojet.

TURBOJET ENGINE

A turbojet engine consists of a compressor that is driven by a shaft connected to a turbine, with a combustion chamber or chambers linking the two. As air is sucked into the engine it is compressed, after which it is passed to the combustion chamber where the fuel is burned. This burning creates a powerful jet of hot gases, which then propels the aircraft forwards.

TURBOPROP ENGINE

A turboprop engine is an engine that uses a jet engine to turn a propeller. The hot jet gases spin the propeller and this creates thrust to power the aircraft forwards.

THRUST

The force produced by a spinning propeller or blasting jet engine that drives an aircraft forwards.

Note to parents and teachers:
Every effort has been made by the Publishers to ensure that the websites in this book are suitable for children, that they are of the highest educational value, and that they contain no inappropriate or offensive material. However, because of the nature of the Internet, it is impossible to guarantee that the contents of these sites will not be altered. We strongly advise that Internet access is supervised by a responsible adult.

INDEX